HAWAII

HELLO
U.S.A.

by Joyce Johnston

Lerner Publications Company

You'll find this picture of Kilauea erupting at the beginning of every chapter of this book. The volcano, located on the island of Hawaii, has been erupting since 1983. In fact, Kilauea is the world's most active volcano. Every minute, 130,000 gallons of lava pour out of its cracks.

Cover (left): Volcanic eruption in Kilauea East Rift, in Hawaii Volcanoes National Park. Cover (right): Waikiki Beach and Diamond Head, on Oahu. Pages 2-3: Musicians and dancers at Waikiki Beach, on Oahu. Page 3: Wailua Falls, on Kauai.

This book is available in two editions:
Library binding by Lerner Publications Company, a division of Lerner Publishing Group
Soft cover by First Avenue Editions, an imprint of Lerner Publishing Group
241 First Avenue North
Minneapolis, MN 55401 U.S.A.

Website address: www.lernerbooks.com

Library of Congress Cataloging-in-Publication Data

Johnston, Joyce, 1958–
    Hawaii / by Joyce Johnston. Rev. and expanded 2nd ed.
      p.   cm. — (Hello U.S.A.)
    Includes index.
    ISBN: 0–8225–4056–8 (lib. bdg. : alk. paper)
    ISBN: 0–8225–4152–1 (pbk. : alk. paper)
    1. Hawaii—Juvenile literature. 2. Hawaii—Geography—Juvenile
literature. I. Title. II. Series.
    DU623.25 .J64 2002
    996.9—dc21   2001000185

Manufactured in the United States of America
1 2 3 4 5 6 – JR – 07 06 05 04 03 02

CONTENTS

Hawaii is famous for its sandy beaches.

THE LAND

Active Islands

I magine leaving the West Coast of the United States on a ship. As the boat cruises toward the southwest, you scan the Pacific Ocean for land. Finally, on the fifth day at sea, islands appear in the distance. After traveling more than 2,400 miles, your ship would reach Hawaii—the southernmost state in the United States.

A chain of 132 islands, Hawaii lies in the middle of the North Pacific Ocean. The chain stretches 1,523 miles northwest from Hawaii Island, the state's largest island.

The Hawaiian Islands began forming millions of years ago when **lava** (hot, liquid rock) oozed from deep within the earth onto the floor of the Pacific Ocean.

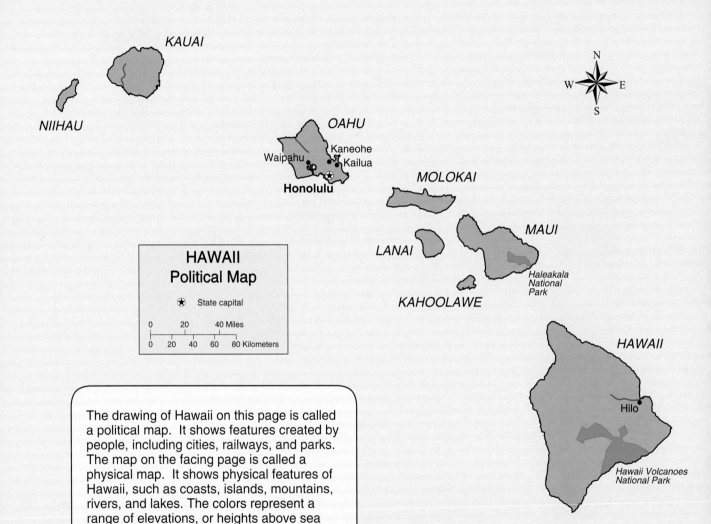

KAUAI

NIIHAU

OAHU

Waipahu   Kaneohe
            Kailua

Honolulu

MOLOKAI

MAUI

LANAI

Haleakala
National
Park

KAHOOLAWE

HAWAII
Political Map

⍟   State capital

0   20   40 Miles

0   20   40   60   80 Kilometers

HAWAII

Hilo

Hawaii Volcanoes
National Park

The drawing of Hawaii on this page is called
a political map. It shows features created by
people, including cities, railways, and parks.
The map on the facing page is called a
physical map. It shows physical features of
Hawaii, such as coasts, islands, mountains,
rivers, and lakes. The colors represent a
range of elevations, or heights above sea
level (see legend box).

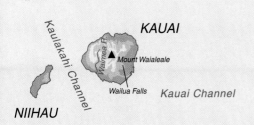

KAUAI

PACIFIC OCEAN

Kaulakahi Channel

Warmea R.

▲ Mount Waialeale

Wailua Falls

Kauai Channel

NIIHAU

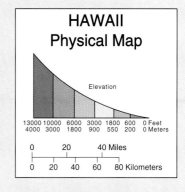
OAHU

Kaiwi Channel

MOLOKAI

N
W   E
S

MAUI

LANAI

Haleakala Crater ▲

KAHOOLAWE

Alenuihaha Channel

HAWAII

Mauna Kea   Akaka Falls

Wailuku R.

Kealakekua Bay

Mauna Loa ▲

Kilauea Crater ▲

PACIFIC OCEAN

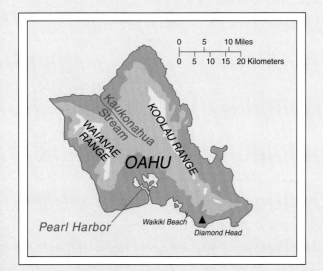

| 0 | 5 | 10 Miles |

| 0 | 5 | 10 | 15 | 20 Kilometers |

Kaukonahua Stream

KOOLAU RANGE

WAIANAE RANGE

OAHU

Pearl Harbor

Waikiki Beach

Diamond Head ▲

The state of Hawaii is made up of islands formed by volcanoes.

The lava cooled, leaving a layer of hardened volcanic rock on the ocean floor. Over the ages, more and more lava trickled from the earth, piling the layers of volcanic rock higher and higher.

While the lava oozed, the ocean floor crept very slowly toward the northwest. The movement pulled the first volcano away from the "hot spot," where the lava was seeping from inside the earth. A new volcano was then created above the hot spot. As these actions were repeated, and the ocean floor shifted, the lava eventually formed a string of volcanoes. One by one, the volcanoes rose above the waves, forming the Hawaiian Islands.

The state is divided into two groups of islands. The first group is made up of 124 small islands, which form the northwestern part of the chain. Wind and water have worn down these islands over time. This process has left only

Coral formations and colorful fish are found in Hawaii's ocean waters.

pieces of volcanic rock and islands made of **coral** (skeletons of small sea animals) and layers of limestone.

The second group consists of eight large islands. Maui and Kahoolawe lie northwest of Hawaii Island. Lanai and Molokai are next in the chain, followed by Oahu, Kauai, and Niihau.

Streams, ocean waves, and winds have shaped Hawaii's rugged, volcanic mountains. The highest peak in the state is Mauna Kea, an inactive volcano. It rises 13,796 feet above sea level near the center of Hawaii Island. Two of the other volcanoes on Hawaii Island—Mauna Loa and Kilauea—still erupt.

Although Hawaii is mountainous, flatlands and lowlands spread over parts of the state. Hawaii's lowlands include the coastal plain of Molokai Island and a wide valley on Maui. On Oahu a broad **plateau** (flat highland) separates the Koolau and Waianae mountain ranges. Farmers raise livestock or plant sugarcane, pineapples, and other crops in these areas.

Cropland spreads out on both sides of the Hanalei River on Kauai Island.

In a few of the state's dry spots, hikers may spot a silversword plant *(right)*. Mauna Kea *(below)*, an inactive volcano, often gets enough snow during the winter for skiing.

The bark of the painted eucalyptus—one of the many trees found in Hawaii's tropical rain forests—is a rainbow of color.

In general, temperatures on the islands are warm and remain fairly constant throughout the year. In the lowlands, temperatures average 77° F in July and 71° F in January.

Steady breezes known as the trade winds bring cooling weather and rainstorms. These storms drop most of their moisture on the northeastern side of the islands. Up to 400 inches of rain fall each year in the state's mountain rain forests. But some valleys and lowlands on the southwestern side of the islands receive 10 inches or less of rain annually.

While violent storms are rare, hurricanes sometimes hit the islands between the months of June and November. During the winter months, the trade winds may stop and southern winds known as *kona* may bring hot, sticky air and storms. Only on Hawaii's highest mountaintops are temperatures cold enough for snow.

Only a few short rivers flow across the islands. The longest of these waterways are the Kaukonahua Stream on Oahu, the Wailuku River on Hawaii Island, and the Waimea River on Kauai.

The *nene,* Hawaii's state bird *(below),* lives on the islands of Maui and Hawaii. Orchids *(right)* and thousands of other tropical flowers cover the hillsides of Hawaii.

Colorful mushrooms grow throughout Hawaii.

Hawaii's warm and humid climate makes the state a natural greenhouse, where many different kinds of plants thrive. Orchids, hibiscus, and other flowering plants that need a lot of moisture bloom on the rainy side of the islands. In the state's rain forests, some ferns reach 40 feet in height, with stems as thick as tree trunks. Cactuses and other desert plants are found in drier areas.

Only two types of mammals—the hoary bat and the monk seal—are native to Hawaii. But the islands are known for their many kinds of birds and sea creatures. Birds such as honeycreepers, which are found only in Hawaii, inhabit the rain forests. The state's underwater treasures include colorful fish darting among coral reefs, sea turtles paddling below the ocean waves, and humpback whales slapping the water with their tails.

THE HISTORY

Pacific Crossroads

H awaii is just one of many groups of islands in a vast region of the Pacific Ocean known as Polynesia. The people who have lived in this part of the world for thousands of years are called Polynesians. The name means "people of the many islands."

Ancient Polynesians were expert navigators. They explored immense stretches of ocean in sailboats, which they made by lashing two huge canoes together and raising a sail. The Polynesian sailors used the stars, clouds, ocean currents, and even seabirds to find their way from island to island.

In about A.D. 300, Polynesians from the Marquesas Islands loaded their canoes with seeds, food, and livestock. They sailed north, carrying their cargo, as well as a few rats that had sneaked onto the boats.

When asking special favors of their gods, ancient Polynesians placed offerings on rock carvings.

Polynesian sailors could travel thousands of miles in oceangoing canoes. The biggest canoes, which were used in warfare and long-distance travel, could carry as many as 200 people.

After traveling 2,000 miles, the sailors discovered a group of islands. They called the land Hawaiki, a name the Polynesians also used to refer to their ancient Asian homeland. Most historians believe that the state of Hawaii takes its name from this word.

About 600 years later, another group of Polynesians sailed to Hawaii from the Pacific island of Tahiti. Both of these groups of ancient Hawaiians worshiped many gods. The islanders believed that their chiefs, or *alii*, were related to these gods.

Makaainana, or ordinary Hawaiians, performed everyday tasks. The men grew coconuts, sweet potatoes, bananas, and sugarcane. They also prepared *poi*, a puddinglike dish made from the taro plant. Some makaainana men collected colorful feathers for decorating the capes and helmets of the alii. Others chopped down *koa* trees and carved the logs into canoes. Women cared for children, tended gardens, and made clothing.

To make *tapa* cloth, Hawaiian women beat tree bark into soft, pulpy strips that can be sewn together.

Fiery lava from Kilauea creeps across a road.

Pele's Volcano

Ancient Hawaiian religious beliefs were based on respect for the powers of nature. Many different gods represented these forces. Hawaiians worshiped some of their gods in the form of idols, or images, made of feathers, wood, stones, shells, and human hair. Trained storytellers told the tales of the gods' lives to a circle of listeners, who were forbidden to move once the sacred story had begun.

Among the most important Hawaiian gods were Ku (the god of war), Kane (the god of life,) Lono (the god of the harvest), and Pele (the goddess of fire). Hawaiians believed that Pele lived at Kilauea volcano on the island of Hawaii. They thought she was responsible for Kilauea's lava flows and anything else related to heat and fire. Prayers to Pele are still said when a new *imu*, or underground oven, is built.

And park rangers at Hawaii Volcanoes National Park on the island of Hawaii receive packages every year from tourists who have taken volcanic rocks from Kilauea as souvenirs. These vacationers return the rocks to the park, claiming that bad luck followed them the minute they took the souvenirs from Pele's volcano.

The *hula*, originally a form of worship, was performed only by highly trained men. According to Hawaiian beliefs, a god named Laka taught men how to do the hula.

Rules called *kapu* guided daily life. For example, makaainana could not let their shadows touch the shadow of an alii. Women were not allowed to eat certain foods or to share meals with men. The punishment for breaking a kapu was often death.

Until the late 1700s, the rest of the world didn't know that Hawaii existed. One night in 1778, two Hawaiian fishers spotted what looked like two islands floating off the coast of Kauai Island. The men quickly paddled to shore to tell others what they had seen. In the morning, people gathered on the beach. The floating islands were actually two large ships.

The ships carried Captain James Cook, a British officer, and his crew. Cook and his men were searching for the Northwest Passage, a water route thought to lead from Europe to Asia.

Although Cook did not stay in Hawaii for long, he and his crew returned later that year to collect food and water. The Hawaiians celebrated the return with parties and feasts that lasted for several weeks. But during their stay, the British ate most of the Hawaiians' food and unknowingly broke many kapu. When the British ships finally left, the Hawaiians were glad to see their visitors go.

The explorers didn't get very far. After a storm damaged their ships, the British returned to Hawaii for repairs. This time, the Hawaiians were not happy to see the sailors and threw rocks at the returning ships.

Because Captain Cook landed during a sacred festival, Hawaiians thought he was a god and offered him gifts.

Artist John Webber traveled with Cook and his crew to record events. He painted this picture of the captain's death.

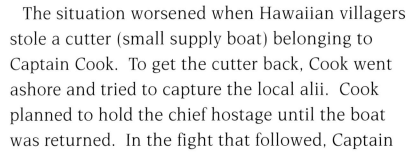

On June 11, Hawaiians celebrate King Kamehameha Day. They place flower necklaces called *leis* on the statue of Kamehameha I, which stands in Kapaau on Hawaii Island.

The situation worsened when Hawaiian villagers stole a cutter (small supply boat) belonging to Captain Cook. To get the cutter back, Cook went ashore and tried to capture the local alii. Cook planned to hold the chief hostage until the boat was returned. In the fight that followed, Captain Cook and several Hawaiians were killed.

At the time of Cook's death, Hawaii was ruled by four alii. But in the 1780s, Kamehameha I—the ruling chief of Hawaii Island—fought for control of all the islands in a lengthy war. By 1810 Kamehameha had defeated the other alii and had united the islands.

During Kamehameha's rule, the Kingdom of Hawaii began to trade with other countries. Workers cut down Hawaii's sandalwood forests and shipped the trees to China. The Chinese, who treasured the sweet-smelling wood, called Hawaii the land of "fragrant mountains."

Hawaii also became an important rest stop for sailors from all over the world. Ships carrying furs from the United States to China anchored in Hawaii's waters. Whaling ships stopped in Hawaii for repairs and supplies. For many years, Hawaiians earned more money from providing whalers and traders with goods than from any other business. These ships brought more than money and goods. The sailors carried diseases, such as measles and cholera, to Hawaii. Because the islanders had never been exposed to these illnesses, thousands of Hawaiians died.

Whales were hunted for their blubber, or fat, which was cooked to produce oil that fueled lamps. Whalebone was used in making a variety of items, including fishing rods and umbrellas.

More changes came to the islands after Kamehameha's son Liholiho became king of Hawaii in 1819. The new king ruled the islands along with Kaahumanu, one of Kamehameha's wives. She persuaded Liholiho to end all kapu. This meant the Hawaiians no longer had to fear death for breaking rules. When the kapu ended, many islanders stopped worshiping Hawaiian gods.

At about the same time, outsiders came to teach Hawaiians a new religion—Christianity. In 1820 a group of **missionaries** who came from the United States landed on Hawaii Island. At first most Hawaiians did not like the new religion because of its strict rules. But after Kaahumanu adopted the missionaries' religion, many other Hawaiians also accepted Christianity.

The missionaries changed Hawaiian life in many ways. They created an alphabet so that Hawaiians could read and write the Hawaiian language. The missionaries opened schools and libraries and built hospitals and churches.

The Hawaiian Language

For hundreds of years, Hawaiians passed on their history and beliefs by singing special chants and telling stories aloud. No written language existed until American missionaries arrived in the early 1800s. The missionaries developed a 12-letter Hawaiian alphabet that included five vowels (a,e,i,o,u) and seven consonants (h,k,l,m,n,p,w). These letters matched the sounds of the spoken Hawaiian language.

Modern written Hawaiian is very different from the original spoken language. Honolulu, for example, was probably once pronounced "Honoruru." But because the missionaries didn't always understand or respect the local pronunciation, they chose a spelling that matched what they thought they heard.

While the island of Niihau is the only place where Hawaiian is commonly spoken, there is a growing interest in learning the language. Some older Hawaiians throughout the state still speak the language at home, and many schools have classes to teach the Hawaiian language to children. Some churches offer services in Hawaiian.

aloha (ah-LOH-hah)	hello; good-bye
alohaaina (ah-LOH-hah-ah-EE-nah)	love of the land
haole (HOW-lee)	white person; mainlander
kupuna (koo-POO-nah)	grandparents
mahalo (mah-HAH-loh)	thank you
ohana (oh-HAHN-nah)	family
pau (PAH-oo)	finished; over

But the missionaries also banned many Hawaiian traditions, such as performing the hula dance and making colorful flower necklaces called *leis.* Hawaiians, who were used to wearing very little in the hot climate, were forced to wear heavy European-style clothing. Those who became Christians could not smoke, drink liquor, fly kites, box, or wrestle.

Still other outsiders followed the missionaries to Hawaii. In 1835 an American firm called Ladd and Company rented land on Kauai Island to start a sugarcane **plantation.** More of these large, privately owned farms were eventually established on other islands. In the next 40 years, sugar became the biggest industry in Hawaii.

After missionaries banned the hula, the dance almost disappeared. In the 1880s, King Kalakaua formed a hula troupe to revive the original dances, many of which are still performed.

Most plantation owners came from the United States and Europe. They hired Hawaiians to plant sugarcane, crush the stalks, and boil the juice that produced sugar. The sugar laborers worked 10-hour days, six days a week, for very low wages.

When Hawaiians refused to work under these conditions, planters brought in laborers from other countries. In exchange for their passage to Hawaii, the laborers signed contracts agreeing to work on the sugar plantations for a certain number of years. They, too, worked long hours for low pay.

Farm laborers spent long hours working in Hawaii's sugarcane fields.

Japanese immigrants came to Hawaii to work in the sugarcane fields.

Hoping to earn more money than they could in their homelands, thousands of Chinese and Japanese **immigrants** came to Hawaii as sugar laborers in the mid-1800s. Smaller numbers of German, Portuguese, and Norwegian workers arrived later.

Some sugar laborers left Hawaii as soon as their contracts were over. But many of them stayed.

They married Hawaiians and opened restaurants or small shops. By 1886 immigrants and people of mixed heritage outnumbered native Hawaiians.

The arrival of people from so many different cultures changed Hawaii. Asians built temples and shrines where they could practice their religions. Hawaiian, Japanese, Chinese, Portuguese, and English words mixed to form a new language—pidgin—that everyone could use.

White residents worried about the increasing number of Asians in Hawaii. They were afraid that Asians might pass laws that white people would dislike. To prevent this from happening, several powerful white businesspeople tried to change Hawaii's government.

In 1887 these business owners pressured King Kalakaua to change Hawaii's election laws. Under the new rules, only men who owned $3,000 worth of land and earned at least $600 each year could vote. Sugar planters and other business owners were the only voters who were that rich. They became the only people to elect government officials.

Although Liliuokalani (*above*) was Hawaii's first queen, she was its last monarch, or royal leader. After trying unsuccessfully to take back control of the kingdom, she was sent to prison (*above right*).

When King Kalakaua died in 1891, his sister, Liliuokalani, became the first queen of Hawaii. Liliuokalani wanted to stop the wealthy white business owners from having so much control over Hawaii. But in 1893, before she could make many changes, a small group of planters and other businesspeople overthrew the queen.

Most Hawaiians supported Liliuokalani. But they didn't have enough soldiers or guns to fight the U.S. Marines, who came ashore to help overthrow the queen. Liliuokalani's arrest ended the rule of kings and queens in Hawaii.

A crowd gathered on August 12, 1898, in Honolulu at Iolani Palace—the former Hawaiian royal residence—to watch the raising of the American flag. The event marked the formal takeover of Hawaii by the United States.

After the overthrow of Queen Liliuokalani, Sanford Dole *(center)* became the new president of the new Republic of Hawaii. Dole was appointed its first governor when Hawaii became a U.S. territory in 1900.

Sanford Dole, the son of U.S. missionaries, led Hawaii's new government. In 1898 Dole reached an agreement with the United States for **annexation** of Hawaii, making it a possession of the United States. On June 14, 1900, Hawaii became a U.S. territory. All islanders—except for Asians not born in Hawaii—became U.S. citizens.

Residents of the Territory of Hawaii paid taxes to the U.S. government, but they could not vote for president or for their own governor. To get these rights, Hawaii needed to become a state. But the U.S. government refused to grant statehood to a territory like Hawaii, where less than half of the population was white.

In the late 1930s, war broke out in Europe and in Asia. The United States tried to stay out of the conflict. But on December 7, 1941, Japanese planes bombed the U.S. naval base at Pearl Harbor on the island of Oahu.

More than 2,400 of Hawaii's soldiers and residents died in the attack. The raiders destroyed almost 200 U.S. military airplanes and sank several warships. Angered by the attack, the United States declared war on Japan and joined World War II.

Fearing a Japanese invasion, the U.S. military immediately took over the Territory of Hawaii. For almost four years, the army controlled many parts of everyday life, from collecting trash to caring for the sick in hospitals to running Hawaii's courts of law. Thousands of U.S. soldiers and other military workers were stationed in Hawaii, and the territory's population nearly doubled.

... we here highly resolve that these dead shall not have died in vain ...

REMEMBER DEC. 7th!

Wartime posters reminded Americans why the United States entered World War II.

The Japanese attack on Pearl Harbor in 1941 left this airfield in smoke and flames.

At the time of the Pearl Harbor attack, more than one-third of Hawaii's residents had ancestors from Japan. The U.S. government feared these people would spy for Japan or join a Japanese invasion of the islands. So the U.S. military arrested many Japanese Americans in Hawaii and closed Japanese schools and radio stations.

Although Japanese Americans were angered by these actions, they were determined to prove their loyalty to the country they considered home—the United States. The men in the 442nd Regimental Combat Team, most of whom were Japanese Americans from Hawaii, won more medals for bravery than any other battalion in World War II.

Senator Daniel K. Inouye served in the 442nd Regimental Combat Team during World War II. He stands in front of a flag that carries the battalion's motto, "Go for Broke."

After the war ended in 1945, Hawaii was on its way to statehood. The government of Hawaii wrote a **constitution** (set of basic laws) that was approved by the territory's voters in 1950. The U.S. government could no longer refuse statehood, when the territory's people had shown heroism and great loyalty to the nation. On August 21, 1959, Hawaii became the 50th state.

Hawaii has changed since it became a state. People of Hawaiian and Asian ancestry have gained some of the powers that Queen Liliuokalani wanted for them. The state's first-ever U.S. representative, Daniel Inouye, is Japanese American. Inouye became a U.S. senator in 1963. In 1985 the people of Hawaii elected the state's first native Hawaiian governor, John Waihee III.

John Waihee III

But many Hawaiians are still angry that U.S. marines helped overthrow Liliuokalani more than 100 years ago. Some native Hawaiians want the islands to become an independent country once again. Others want the U.S. government to recognize their status as a separate nation within the United States.

The state of Hawaii is looking for ways to repay native Hawaiians for the country they lost when Liliuokalani was overthrown. At the same time, the state continues to welcome the many groups of people who call the islands home.

Diamond Head, an inactive volcano, towers over Honolulu's skyscrapers. More than 370,000 people live in Hawaii's biggest city.

PEOPLE & ECONOMY

The Aloha State

In the Hawaiian language, the word *aloha* can mean both "hello" and "good-bye." Aloha also expresses a feeling of affection or love for other people. Hawaii earned its nickname, the Aloha State, from this ancient tradition of friendliness.

Hawaii's hospitality, natural beauty, and warm climate have made tourism the state's most valuable industry. Each year the Aloha State welcomes more than 6 million tourists, who spend about $11 billion during their stay. Most visitors come from the mainland United States or from Japan and other Asian countries.

British sailors gave Diamond Head on Oahu Island its name because they thought diamonds covered the volcano's slopes.

Hawaii's many service workers include tour guides *(left, standing)* and instructors *(below)* at the Polynesian Cultural Center on Oahu.

The workers who help tourists in Hawaii have service jobs. These service workers include helicopter pilots who fly visitors over Hawaii's coastal beaches and lush, green valleys. Tour guides in Honolulu show visitors the Chinese temples and noodle factories of the city's Chinatown neighborhood.

Other service workers in Hawaii stock shelves in grocery stores, drive ambulances, or sell houses. Teachers, nurses, and doctors also hold service jobs.

The U.S. military has bases in Hawaii for each of its service branches. Here, marines take part in a combat readiness exercise.

Altogether, 68 percent of Hawaii's workers have service jobs helping other people or businesses.

The government and military employ 22 percent of the Hawaiian workforce. Both military personnel and civilians work on the U.S. army, air force, navy, and marine bases on Oahu.

About 4 percent of the Hawaiian workforce earn a living from construction jobs. Some of these workers build hotels, stores, and restaurants in the state's cities and tourist areas.

Only 3 percent of Hawaii's workers have agricultural jobs. Some farmers grow coffee, macadamia nuts, bananas, papayas, or avocados. Others raise hogs, chickens, or dairy cattle. Livestock and livestock products contribute about 15 percent of farm income. Some growers cultivate orchids and other flowers, many of which are shipped overseas to be sold.

Crops provide about 85 percent of Hawaii's farming income. Forty percent of the money Hawaii earns from agriculture comes from sugarcane and pineapples, which grow only in tropical climates. The island of Maui produces most of Hawaii's sugarcane, as well as most of its pineapples.

Beef cattle are raised on some of Hawaii's farms.

The pineapples and sugarcane grown in Hawaii are sent to the state's factories, where about 3 percent of Hawaii's workers have jobs. Laborers in these factories slice and can pineapples and crush sugarcane for juice to make sugar. Then workers send the products off to other parts of the world.

Food processing is the biggest manufacturing industry in Hawaii, but workers also make bread, soft drinks, clothing, magazines, books, newspapers, and stone, clay, and glass products. On Oahu, workers at oil refineries process petroleum.

Hawaii's 1,000 factories earn about $1 billion for the state. Most of the factories are located in Honolulu and other cities on Oahu, or near Hilo.

Pineapples are one of Hawaii's main agricultural products.

KAUAI

NIIHAU

OAHU

MOLOKAI

LANAI

MAUI

KAHOOLAWE

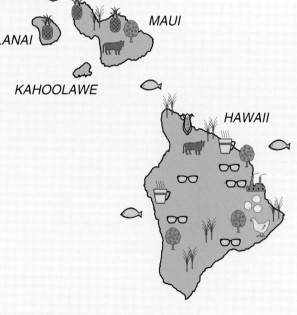

HAWAII

HAWAII
Economic Map

The symbols on this map show where different economic activities take place in Hawaii. The legend below explains what each symbol stands for.

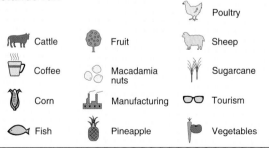

				Poultry
Cattle		Fruit		Sheep
Coffee		Macadamia nuts		Sugarcane
Corn		Manufacturing		Tourism
Fish		Pineapple		Vegetables

47

The people of Hawaii come from many different backgrounds.

Oahu is home to most of the state's residents. Honolulu, Hawaii's capital and its largest city, sits on the southeastern corner of Oahu. About one-third of Hawaii's 1.2 million people live in Honolulu.

Hawaii's other major cities are much smaller than Honolulu. Hilo, with nearly 41,000 residents, is located on Hawaii Island. Kailua, Kaneohe, Waipahu—each with fewer than 37,000 people—are located on Oahu.

Many of Hawaii's residents or their ancestors came to the islands from other parts of the world. About 30 per-cent of Hawaiians have European ancestors. Another 25 percent have Japanese ancestors. People of native Hawaiian ancestry make up about 15 percent of the state's residents.

Most of Hawaii's other residents have ancestors who came to the state from China, the Philippines, Korea, Samoa, and Southeast Asia. About 7 percent of Hawaiians are Latinos. African Americans and American Indians make up only a small part of the state's population.

Native Hawaiians are not the largest ethnic group in Hawaii, but their culture is an important part of Hawaiian life. Two well-known Hawaiian traditions are the hula, which means "dance" in the Hawaiian language, and the *luau*, a feast of Hawaiian food and dancing. Many hula performers wear traditional skirts made from the leaves of *ti* plants. The dancers move their arms, hands, hips, and feet to a *mele*, or chant, that tells a story.

Two friends *(above)* enjoy a day at the beach. A young girl *(right)* performs a traditional Japanese festival dance.

Traditional Hawaiian musical instruments, such as the *pahu* (a large drum), accompany the dancers. At a luau, cooks roast a whole pig in an underground oven. Guests fill banana-leaf plates with pork, sweet potatoes, poi, and other Hawaiian foods.

The ocean is Hawaii's playground. Sailors glide from island to island with the trade winds. Below the water's surface, snorkelers and scuba divers can see a rainbow of colorful fish and more than 1,000 different kinds of glittering seashells. *Heenalu*, or wave sliding, is an ancient Hawaiian sport also known as surfing. Professional surfers ride the big waves each year at the Hawaii Pro Surfing Championships on Oahu.

On land, residents and visitors enjoy golf, tennis, volleyball, hiking, horseback riding, and football. One of the state's best-known teams, the University of Hawaii's Rainbow Warriors, plays other college football teams from around the United States. A Rainbow Warrior might be selected to compete at the Hula Bowl, a college all-star football game held each January in Honolulu.

A luau hostess wearing a lei welcomes her guests.

Nature's Necklace

When people arrive on or leave the Hawaiian Islands, they are usually presented with a lei. These beautiful flower necklaces are worn at many other occasions as well, including weddings. Historically, Hawaiians gave leis to their local alii, or chief, as a sign of affection. Warring chiefs who wanted to make peace sat down to weave a lei together.

Leis are made by stringing, sewing, or braiding together more than just flowers. Leaves, shells, nuts, seaweed, ferns, and other greenery are also commonly used. Each island has its own unique lei. For example, Hawaii's lei is made from the red *lehua* blossom, while Molokai's is fashioned from the green leaves and white flowers of the *kukui* tree.

Hawaii's two national parks attract many visitors. At Haleakala National Park on Maui, adventurous hikers can walk into Haleakala Crater, an inactive volcano. The trail to the top of Mauna Loa at Hawaii Volcanoes National Park on Hawaii Island leads hikers past rare birds and hardened lava flows. From the Crater Rim Trail, which circles Kilauea volcano, visitors can look out over the volcano to see for themselves how Hawaii was born.

Cinder cones, formed from chunks of volcanic rock, rise as high as 600 feet in the crater of Haleakala volcano on Maui.

Wild pigs are a threat to their forest homes.

Alien mammals such as pigs killed many of Hawaii's trees by digging up the roots and by eating the bark. Goats and cattle trampled or ate many native plants, which had not developed thorns, bad-tasting leaves, or other features to protect against grazing animals.

Mosquitoes, which came to Hawaii on trading ships in the 1800s, spread deadly diseases to Hawaii's birds. Dogs, mongooses, and rats attacked birds that built their nests on the ground. The mynah bird, which was brought to Hawaii from India in 1865, stole the nests of Hawaii's birds and competed with them for food.

Hawaii's forests are also threatened by the construction of hotels, beach clubs, condominiums, and other buildings.

The destruction of Hawaii's forests has also been deadly to the state's plants and animals. The early Polynesians burned down forests to create farmland. Over the years, farmers have continued to turn woodlands into cropland.

Tourism has also hurt Hawaii's forests. Builders have cut down trees and filled swamps and other wetlands to put up hotels and to create roads. By the 1990s, about two-thirds of Hawaii's original forests, including almost half of the state's rain forests, were gone. Without the forests, many of the unique life-forms that depend on these areas for shelter and food cannot survive.

The people of Hawaii are working to save endangered plants and animals. Scientists at captive-breeding facilities such as the Keahou (Hawaii Island) and Maui Bird Conservation Centers raise families of endangered animals such as the nene (Hawaiian goose). Researchers at botanical gardens are growing some of Hawaii's rarest plants. The plants will eventually be transplanted into areas where they cannot be disturbed by animals or people.

Hawaii has spent millions of dollars building fences to keep wild pigs and other alien species out of the state's forests. Environmental organizations are asking the government to prevent businesses from building in and polluting forests, wetlands, and other areas that are home to endangered plants and animals. Hawaii has also passed strict laws to keep people from bringing alien species into the state.

Hawaii's residents and visitors can help save the state's endangered plants and animals by leaving them alone. Pet owners are encouraged to keep their pets from running free so that the animals can't eat or tear up native plants or kill Hawaii's birds.

The millions of people who visit Hawaii can help save endangered species by leaving their pets and any other alien animals or plants at home. Hikers from outside Hawaii can clean their boots to make sure their footgear doesn't spread alien seeds in Hawaii's forests. If everyone pitches in, Hawaii's wildlife has a chance to survive.

A tall fence helps keep wild pigs out of Haleakala National Park.

ALL ABOUT HAWAII

Fun Facts

Surfing was invented thousands of years ago by the Polynesian peoples who first settled Hawaii. They rode ocean waves on carved wooden boards that weighed more than 150 pounds and measured up to 20 feet in length. Modern surfboards are made of plastic and fiberglass, weigh about 12 pounds, and are only 6 feet long.

Hawaii is the only state completely made up of islands. It is also the only state where you'll find coffee plantations and tropical rain forests.

Mount Waialeale on Hawaii's Kauai Island is one of the wettest spots on earth. The 5,080-foot mountain receives more than 460 inches of rain each year.

Mauna Loa, on the island of Hawaii, is the world's largest volcano. Mauna Loa rises 31,784 feet, but less than half of its height is actually above sea level.

Every year more than 1.5 million people view the remains of the USS *Arizona* at Pearl Harbor. The warship and its crew were bombed by Japan during a surprise raid on the naval base on December 7, 1941.

In the 1960s, astronauts trained for moon voyages by walking on Mauna Loa's cooled and hardened lava fields, which resemble the surface of the moon.

Hawaii was once an independent monarchy, ruled by kings and queens. It's the only state that ever had this form of government. Hawaii's kings and queens lived in Iolani Palace, the only royal residence in the United States.

STATE SONG

"Hawai'i Pono'i" was written in 1874, when Hawaii was an
independent kingdom. King Kalakaua wrote the words, and
Henry Berger, the royal bandmaster, wrote the music.

HAWAI'I PONO'I

Words by King Kalakaua
Music by Henry Berger

You can hear "Hawai'i Pono'i" by visiting this website:
<http://www.50states.com/songs/hawaii.htm>

A HAWAIIAN RECIPE

Haupia is Hawaiian coconut pudding.
It is a traditional dessert at luaus,
where it is cut into small squares and
served on leaves from the ti plant.
This simple dessert is especially
good with a sauce or salad made of
tropical fruits such as kiwi,
mango, and papaya.

HAUPIA

5 tablespoons ground arrowroot (found in the spice section of your supermarket), or 6
   tablespoons cornstarch
6 tablespoons sugar
3 cups canned coconut milk
2 teaspoons vanilla extract

1. Mix arrowroot or cornstarch and sugar in saucepan.
2. Slowly add coconut milk and vanilla extract. Heat on medium until mixture is bubbling
   slightly.
3. Stir constantly (to avoid lumps) until it thickens.
4. Pour into an 8-inch square cake pan and chill until set, for about four hours.
5. When you're ready to serve it, slice the haupia into two-inch squares.

Serves 6–9 people.

HISTORICAL TIMELINE

A.D. 300 Polynesians from the Marquesas Islands arrive in the Hawaiian Islands.

900 Polynesians from Tahiti settle in Hawaii.

1778 British explorer James Cook lands on Kauai.

1780s Kamehameha I fights for control of all the islands.

1810 Kamehameha I unifies the Kingdom of Hawaii.

1819 King Liholiho, Kamehameha's son, ends all kapu.

1820 American missionaries sail to Hawaii.

1835 Ladd and Company founds the first permanent sugarcane plantation in Hawaii at Koloa on Kauai.

mid-1800s Chinese and Japanese immigrants move to Hawaii to work on sugarcane plantations.

1874 King Kalakaua, the Merry Monarch, becomes king. Hawaiian music, the hula, and other old Hawaiian customs regain popularity.

1885 The pineapple industry begins in Hawaii after Jamaican pineapple plants are imported.

1887 White business owners pressure King Kalakaua to change Hawaiian election laws.

1893 Queen Liliuokalani is overthrown by U.S. Marines.

1898 The United States annexes Hawaii.

1900 Hawaii becomes a U.S. territory.

1941 Japan attacks Pearl Harbor during World War II.

1959 Hawaii becomes the 50th state.

1985 John Waihee III is the first native Hawaiian elected as governor.

1993 Hawaiians mark the 100th anniversary of the overthrow of Liliuokalani.

1998 Democrat Benjamin Cayetano is elected to a second term as Hawaii's fifth governor.

OUTSTANDING HAWAIIANS

Akebono

Akebono (born 1970) is a 466-pound sumo wrestler. Born Chad Rowan in Waimanalo, Hawaii, Akebono moved to Japan in 1988 to learn the popular Japanese sport. Five years later, he became the first non-Japanese wrestler to rise to *yokozuna*, sumo's highest rank.

Tia Carrere

Tia Carrere (born 1967) played Wayne's rock-star girlfriend in the movie *Wayne's World*. A native of Honolulu, Carrere released her first album, *Dream*, in 1993. She has also starred in the movies *Rising Sun*, *Wayne's World 2*, and *True Lies*.

Benjamin Cayetano (born 1939) was the first Filipino American to be elected state governor. Raised in Honolulu, he earned a law degree and went on to serve in the Hawaii House of Representatives and in the state senate. He served as lieutenant governor before being elected governor in 1994. He was reelected in 1998.

James Dole

James Dole (1877–1958), the man behind Dole pineapple products, moved to Hawaii in 1899. He opened a cannery and then began shipping the first canned pineapple to the U.S. mainland. Dole's success encouraged others to grow the fruit, which became Hawaii's second-largest industry.

Hiram Fong (born 1906) is a lawyer and businessman who became the first American of Chinese heritage to be elected to the U.S. Senate. The Honolulu native served three terms, which ran from 1959 to 1977.

Hiram Fong

Mamoru Funai (born 1932) writes and illustrates children's books. Among his award-winning books are *Moke and Poki in the Rain Forest* and *On a Picnic.* Funai is from Kauai.

Mamoru Funai

Don Ho (born 1930) is a singer and nightclub entertainer from Honolulu. In the 1970s, he hosted *The Don Ho Show*, a television program featuring music from Hawaii. Ho is best known for his song "Tiny Bubbles."

Charlie Hough (born 1948) is a pitcher from Honolulu. Playing for the Texas Rangers from 1982 to 1988, Hough was named Greatest Pitcher in (Ranger) Franchise History. A three-time World Series pitcher, he joined the Florida Marlins in 1993. Hough was the Los Angeles Dodgers' pitching coach from 1998 to 1999.

Charlie Hough

Daniel K. Inouye (born 1924), from Honolulu, was the first Japanese American to be elected to the U.S. Congress. After serving in World War II, he studied law and eventually entered politics. Inouye was elected to the U.S. House of Representatives in 1959. He began serving in the U.S. Senate in 1963.

Duke Paoa Kahanamoku (1890–1968) was a surfer who helped make the sport popular around the world. Also a champion swimmer, he won gold medals in the 100-meter freestyle event at the 1912 and 1920 Olympic Games. Kahanamoku was born in Honolulu.

Duke Paoa Kahanamoku

Kamehameha I (1758?–1819) became king of Hawaii in 1795. His family ruled the Kingdom of Hawaii until 1872, when Kamehameha V died, leaving no heirs. Kamehameha I was born in Kohala, Hawaii.

Kamehameha I

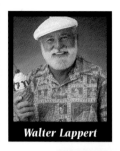

Walter Lappert

Liliuokalani

Bette Midler

Patsy Mink

Walter Lappert (born 1921), a businessman originally from Austria, retired to Kauai, where he opened an ice cream shop in 1983. Using Hawaiian ingredients such as guavas and mangoes to make unique flavors of ice cream, he turned a small store into a $15 million business.

Liliuokalani (1838–1917), Hawaii's last monarch, became queen in 1891 after the death of King Kalakaua, her brother. Liliuokalani tried to strengthen the power of the monarchy but was overthrown in 1893 by a small group of U.S. Marines. Born in Honolulu, she wrote "Aloha Oe," Hawaii's traditional song of farewell.

Lois Lowry (born 1937), an award-winning children's book author, created the popular character Anastasia Krupnik. Lowry won a Newbery Medal in 1990 for *Number the Stars* and again in 1994 for *The Giver.* She is a native of Honolulu.

Bette Midler (born 1945) is an actress, singer, and Broadway performer. Raised in Honolulu, she has starred in several films, including *Beaches* and *The First Wives' Club.* Among her musical hits are the album *The Divine Miss M* and the song "Wind Beneath My Wings," both of which have won Grammy Awards.

Patsy Mink (born 1927), a lawyer and professor from Paia, Hawaii, was elected to the state senate in 1959. She went on to serve in the U.S. House of Representatives from 1965 to 1977. She was reelected to the House of Representatives in 1990.

Ellison Onizuka (1946–1986), born on Hawaii Island, was the first Japanese American to fly in space. He spent eight years with the U.S. Air Force before becoming an astronaut in the late 1970s. Onizuka was on board the space shuttle *Challenger* in 1986 when it exploded shortly after takeoff, killing all crew members.

Ellison Onizuka

William Patterson (1899–1980) built United Airlines into one of the world's largest commercial airlines. Under his leadership, the airline developed equipment that helped make flying safer and became one of the first to hire female flight attendants. Patterson was born in Honolulu.

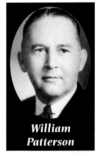

William Patterson

R. C. Leimana Pelton (born 1944) moved to Hawaii in 1980 to create sculptures from molten lava. He works near Hawaii Island's Kilauea volcano, shoveling lava into molds placed in trashcans, where the sculptures cool and harden. The finished pieces include abstract figures as well as vases and masks.

Richard Smart (1913–1992), from Honolulu, ran the largest private cattle ranch in the United States. Parker Ranch, founded on Hawaii Island in 1847 by Smart's great-great-great-grandfather, grew to the size of 225,000 acres under Smart's leadership.

Richard Smart

John Waihee III (born 1946) was the first person of native Hawaiian descent to be elected governor of Hawaii. A lawyer, Waihee also served in the Hawaii House of Representatives and was lieutenant governor of the state. He was governor from 1986 until 1994. Waihee was born in Honokaa.

FACTS-AT-A-GLANCE

Nickname: Aloha State

Song: "Hawai'i Pono'i" ("Hawaii's Own")

Motto: *Ua Mau Ke Ea O Ka Aina I Ka Pono* (The Life of the Land is Perpetuated in Righteousness)

Flower: yellow hibiscus

Tree: kukui

Bird: nene (Hawaiian goose)

Fish: humuhumunukunuku apua'a

Marine mammal: humpback whale

Gem: black coral

Date and ranking of statehood: August 21, 1959, the 50th state

Capital: Honolulu

Area: 6,423 square miles

Rank in area, nationwide: 47th

Average July temperature: 75° F

Average January temperature: 68° F

Hawaii's flag has a small version of Britain's flag in the upper left corner. It honors British captain George Vancouver, who gave Hawaii its first flag in 1794. The eight horizontal stripes represent each of the state's main islands.

POPULATION GROWTH

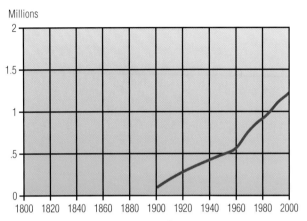

Millions

This chart shows how Hawaii's population has grown from 1900 to 2000.

Hawaii's state seal shows King Kamehameha and the goddess of Liberty holding a shield.

Population: 1,211,537 (2000 census)

Rank in population, nationwide: 42nd

Major cities and populations: (2000 census) Honolulu (371,657), Hilo (40,759), Kailua (36,513), Kaneohe (34,970), Waipahu (33,108)

U.S. senators: 2

U.S. representatives: 2

Electoral votes: 4

Natural resources: forests, groundwater, soil, titanium oxide, volcanic rock

Agricultural products: avocados, bananas, cattle, coffee, eggs, flowers and leis, guavas, hogs, macadamia nuts, papayas, pineapples, sugarcane

Fishing industry: bigeye, shellfish, swordfish

Manufactured goods: bread, canned pineapple, clothing, dairy products, glass products, printed materials, refined petroleum, refined sugar, soft drinks, stone products

WHERE HAWAIIANS WORK

Services—68 percent (services include jobs in trade; community, social, and personal services; finance, insurance, and real estate; transportation, communication, and utilities)

Government—22 percent

Construction—4 percent

Manufacturing—3 percent

Agriculture—3 percent

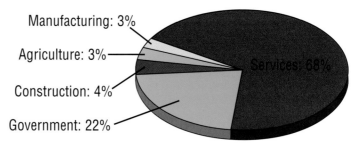

Manufacturing: 3%
Agriculture: 3%
Construction: 4%
Government: 22%
Services: 68%

GROSS STATE PRODUCT

Services—70 percent

Government—22 percent

Construction—4 percent

Manufacturing—3 percent

Agriculture—1 percent

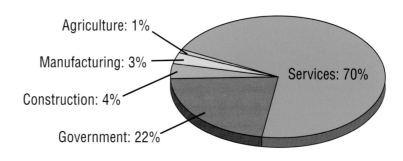

Agriculture: 1%
Manufacturing: 3%
Construction: 4%
Services: 70%
Government: 22%

HAWAII WILDLIFE

Mammals: black-tailed deer, dolphin, Hawaiian hoary bat, Hawaiian monk seal, humpback whale, mongoose, sperm whale, wild pig

Birds: *akepa, akiapolaau, alala* (Hawaiian crow), brown booby, *elepaio,* golden plover, great frigate bird, Hawaiian coot, Hawaiian hawk, honeycreeper, koloa, nene

Amphibians and reptiles: gecko, green sea turtle, hawksbill turtle, leatherback sea turtle

Fish: black-tipped shark, parrotfish, tiger shark, triggerfish, white-tipped shark, yellow butterfly fish

Wild plants: *alulu, awikiwiki,* bougainvillea, heliconia, *loulu,* Mauna Kea silversword, night-blooming cereus, *opuhe, pikake,* plumeria, taro, ti plant, yellow hibiscus

Trees: banyan, baobao, eucalyptus, *hau, kiawe, koa, kukui, ohia*

A green sea turtle passes by a reef near Maui.

PLACES TO VISIT

Akaka Falls State Park on Hawaii
Located near Hilo, Akaka Falls plunges 442 feet into a wooded gorge below.

Barking Sands Beach on Kauai
The sand of this beach becomes so dry that when it is walked on, it makes a sound like a barking dog.

Bishop Museum on Oahu
Founded in 1889, the museum is famous for its displays of the best of Polynesia—textiles, photos, crafts, and more. It also includes several items from the royal Hawaiian collection.

Diamond Head on Oahu
This 760-foot inactive volcanic peak offers a sweeping view across Waikiki Beach and Honolulu.

Haleakala National Park on Maui
Maui's 27,284-acre national park has plenty of sites to see in, on, and around the inactive Haleakala volcano.

Iolani Palace on Oahu
Built in 1882, America's only royal residence was home to King Kalakaua and later his sister, Queen Liliuokalani.

Kalaupapa National Historical Park on Molokai
Once a community for victims of Hansen's disease (leprosy), this tiny village is a national park and a piece of history.

Kealakekua Bay on Hawaii Island

Kealakekua is the site where Captain James Cook was killed in 1779. A monument was built here to honor Cook.

Polynesian Cultural Center on Oahu

At this center near Laie, seven villages represent the people of Fiji, Hawaii, the Marquesas Islands, New Zealand, the Samoa Islands, Tahiti, and Tonga.

USS *Arizona* Memorial on Oahu

Visitors can see the remains of the ship resting at the bottom of the harbor. It sank with more than 1,100 men aboard during the Japanese attack on Pearl Harbor.

Volcanoes National Park on Hawaii Island

Catch a glimpse of the hissing Kilauea volcano, which has been in a state of constant eruption since 1983.

Waimea Canyon on Kauai Shipwreck Beach on Lanai

This beautifully colored gorge on Kauai Shipwreck Beach is about 2,000 feet deep. It was also Captain Cook's first landing site in Hawaii.

A replica of Captain Cook's ship

ANNUAL EVENTS

Hula Bowl on Oahu—*January*

Narcissus Festival on Oahu—*January or February*

Kuhio Day, statewide—*March*

Merrie Monarch Festival on Hawaii—*April*

Lei Day, statewide—*May*

50th State Fair on Oahu—*May–June*

King Kamehameha celebration, statewide—*June*

Makawao Rodeo on Maui—*July*

International Festival of the Pacific on Hawaii—*July*

Hula Festival, Honolulu—*August*

Macadamia Nut Harvest Festival on Hawaii—*August*

Kona Coffee Festival on Hawaii Island—*November*

Hawaiian Pro Surfing Championships on Oahu—*November or December*

GLOSSARY

annexation: adding a country or other territory to another country or state that is usually bigger and more powerful. Annexation can take place peacefully or by military force.

aquifer: an underground layer of rock, sand, or gravel containing water that can be drawn out for use above ground

constitution: the system of basic laws or rules of a government, society, or organization; the document in which these laws or rules are written

coral: rocklike formations made up of the skeletons of small sea animals called coral polyps. Coral is found in warm areas.

immigrant: a person who moves into a foreign country and settles there

lava: hot, melted rock that erupts from a volcano or from cracks in the earth's surface and that hardens as it cools

missionary: a person sent out by a religious group to spread its beliefs to other people

plantation: a large estate, usually in a warm climate, on which crops are grown by workers who live on the estate

plateau: a large, relatively flat area that stands above the surrounding land

INDEX

PHOTO ACKNOWLEDGMENTS

Cover photographs by J.D. Griggs/CORBIS (left), Douglas Peebles/CORBIS (right). Digital Cartographics, pp. 1, 8, 9, 47; Richard T. Nowitz/CORBIS, pp. 2–3; Rick Doyle/CORBIS, p. 3; © G. Brad Lewis/Innerspace Visions, pp. 4 (detail), 7 (detail), 13 (left), 17 (detail, left), 41, 53 (detail, left); © 1995, John Penisten/Pacific Pictures, pp. 6, 12, 17, 19, 20, 24, 45, 46, 49 (bottom); U.S. Geological Survey, p. 10; Cory Williams, p. 11; U.S. Fish and Wildlife Service, p. 13 (inset); Buddy Mays/TRAVEL STOCK, pp. 14, 16 (inset), 42, 43 (both), 49 (top), 52, 54, 60; Kay Shaw Photography, pp. 15 (right), 59; Jack Jeffrey, pp. 15, 53, 55, 57; Hawaii State Archives, pp. 18, 21, 23, 29, 30, 32 (both), 33, 34, 39, 66 (second from bottom), 67 (second from bottom), 67 (bottom), 68 (second from top); Library of Congress, pp. 22, 36; New Bedford Whaling Museum, p. 25; Paul J. Buklarewicz, p. 28; National Archives (neg. #761), p. 35; Senator Daniel Inouye's Office, p. 37; Governor's Office, p. 38; © Andre Seale/Innerspace Visions, p. 40; DoD Still Media Records Center, p. 44; Elaine Little/World Photo Images, p. 48 (both); © Doug Perrine/Innerspace Visions, p. 51; © James D. Watt/Innerspace Visions, p. 56; Dan Lerner, p. 58; Jack Lindstrom, p. 61; Tim Seeley, pp. 63, 71 (top), 72; Reuters/Bettmann, p. 66 (top); Hollywood Book & Poster, p. 66 (second from top), 68 (second from bottom); U.S. Senate Republican Party Committee, p. 66 (bottom); Mamoru Funai, p. 67 (top); Texas Rangers, p. 67 (second from top); Lappert's Hawaii, p. 68 (top); Congresswoman Patsy Mink's Office, p. 68 (bottom); NASA, p. 69 (top); United Airlines, p. 69 (center); Parker Ranch, p. 69 (bottom); Jean Matheny, p. 70; © Michael S. Nolan/Innerspace Visions, p. 73; © Sue Dabritz-Yuen/Innerspace Visions, p. 75; © Dave Homcy/Innerspace Visions, p. 80.